BEYOND THE FACTS
Faith Sees the Deepest Truth

Reflections of a TV News Anchor

by John F. Bachman

Kirk House Publishers
Minneapolis, Minnesota

Beyond the Facts
Faith Sees the Deepest Truths
Reflections of a TV News Anchor
by John F. Bachman

Copyright 2005 Kirk House Publishers All rights reserved. Except for brief quotations in articles or reviews, no part of this book may be reproduced in any manner without prior permission from the publisher.

Design by Jesse Hubbard

Library of Congress Cataloging-in-Publication data

Bachman, John F., 1948
  Beyond the facts : faiths sees the deepest truth : reflections of a TV news anchor / by John F. Bachman
       p. cm.
   ISBN-10: 1-886513-70-8 (perfect bound : alk. paper)
   ISBN-13: 1-798-886513-70-
     1. Meditations. I Bachman, John, 1948

BV4832.3 .B33 2005
262'.12 — dc21
                                       2005043299

Kirk House Publishers, P.O. Box 390759, Minneapolis, MN 55439
Manufactured in the United States of America

Contents

Preface 5

Introduction 7

Society and Culture 13

Sin 39

Fate 53

Inspiration 67

PREFACE

During the course of more than 40 years as a journalist I've often been asked, "How do you personally deal with all the bad news you have to report? Don't you get depressed or cynical?"

It's not an easy question to answer. To say, "No, I am not personally affected. After all, I'm a professional and I have a detachment from the consequences of what I report," is a cold and inhumane reaction. Indeed, I would argue that such a journalist is not emotionally suited to the profession. The best journalists I know are, to one degree or another, empathetic, fully realized men and women who respond to what they're reporting in deeply personal ways. That they don't share their feelings on the air or in print is a tribute to their professional integrity and not a comment on their personal detachment.

As for me, at this stage in my career, after four decades of witnessing cataclysmic change, wrenching personal tragedies on a large scale and small, natural and man-made disasters, I still struggle not just with the consequences but also with the causes. I am constantly in search of answers.

My colleague John Bachman draws on his training in a seminary and a life-time as a committed man of faith to offer this thoughtful and spiritual view of stories he's encountered.

In so doing, he provides a personal and Biblical context for the failures as well as the triumphs of humankind.

It's not unusual for a journalist from time to time to allow a peek into his or her own most deeply held beliefs but those insights are almost always rooted in a political or cultural ideology. What's special, indeed, important, about John Bachman's reflections is that he takes us to a place too seldom associated with journalism: faith.

Journalists and their profession have a fixed image, carefully burnished and nurtured by myth and fact. Hard boiled, hard living cynics who scoff at goodness and celebrate rogues. Like most stereotypes, that one, too, is exaggerated.

Reporters, editors, anchors, camera crews, writers, all the elements of any news organization, represent a wide range of backgrounds, ambitions, motivations and, yes, faiths. It is that full spectrum of experience and belief that shapes who they are and how they personally respond to what they witness. It must not distort what they report but it should not be under-valued as a foundation of their individual integrity and humanity.

I've known John for many years and I have always admired his professional skills and his personal commitment to his family and community. Now I am grateful to him for sharing his faith and his moral clarity in a way that serves as a reminder to journalists and viewers and readers alike that the daily failures and achievements of mankind are not simply fleeting images on the screen or the front page.

Tom Brokaw
NBC Nightly News

INTRODUCTION

Early in my career, while reporting for a television station in Chicago, I covered a particularly horrific fire. Inside a gutted apartment, firefighters found the bodies of two babies. They had been left alone by their mother. While my camera crew and I were still on the scene, the mother returned from a local bar. Bewildered by the fire trucks and police cars and television cameras, she learned that her children had died. There, on that city sidewalk, she screamed hysterically — a scream that stays with me to this day.

Professionally, we had to focus on some basic journalistic questions. In our report, should we include the mother's dreadful grief captured on camera? Did that video invade her privacy? Did it help to tell a compelling and cautionary story? Of course the newscasts that night — as well as conventional wisdom — extended little sympathy to the mother. But days, even weeks later, as I continued to ponder her tragic and seemingly genuine reaction, I couldn't help but believe that God's arms were still open to her. Spiritual reflection — beyond the facts — told me that her searing scream had been heard.

As a broadcast journalist, it's not my job or even privilege to offer spiritual reflections during a newscast. It's hard enough to deliver the facts, to report accurately and fairly when one political statement is debunked minutes later by another, one economic figure contradicted hours later by another.

But privately meditating on the daily news can challenge and enrich personal faith, and help lead us to the profoundly true. An honest and rigorous examination of the factual events can serve as a prism for understanding God's presence in this world. We can't isolate our faith from the realities of today's often chaotic world. Faith and current events must intersect and inform each other. The result can be surprising and meaningful insights — the deepest truths — beyond the facts.

Years ago in the Twin Cities I anchored a newscast on location — at the site of a deadly attack. A gunman had held up a local post office — killing a policeman, wounding two other people, and finally taking his own life. Minutes before we began the broadcast, I scanned the entire scene: our lights and cameras, the police tape and barricades, and the murmuring crowd gathered for the show. The circus-like atmosphere hardly conveyed the private hell to be endured that night by the families of the victims. I was part of the show, but so was the crowd, and in some tangential way so were the viewers at home. We were all disconnected, by the distance of the lens, from actually touching and feeling the horrid truth. Reflection later that night deepened my grasp of the tragic reality shared by those truly involved. The explosive volume of information transmitted electronically can desensitize all of us to the breadth of the human condition — from the depths of suffering to the heights of joy. People of faith can't tolerate that disconnect — we lose sight of our purpose and meaning.

Encounters with two Presidents spoke to me about the challenges of relating our faith to the real world. The first occurred at the White House on the day of the Oklahoma City bombing. Three of us — all news anchors from Des Moines — had been invited to interview President Clinton about an upcoming agricultural conference in Iowa. The bombing occurred while we were flying to Washington, D.C. that morning. As our nation wrestled with this frightening and unprecedented attack inside our own borders, the likelihood of still gaining access to the President that same day seemed remote. But early in the evening, we were ushered into the Roosevelt Room for a nearly hour-long interview. It gave me the chance to question President Clinton about the role his faith played on such a day—a historic day of national crisis and tragedy. He told me in very convincing fashion that he couldn't imagine being President and facing the awesome responsibilities of the office without his faith. He said that after learning of the bombing he had prayed for the victims and their families, and he had prayed for guidance on how he should respond as President. I pursued the topic of faith. I noted how theologian Reinhold Niebuhr had written that the statesman of faith must often choose the lesser of two evils, and that compromise is painfully difficult. An animated Clinton agreed, and then amplified the thought with a reference to sociologist Max Weber's writings. Clinton quoted Weber, saying the statesman of faith in dealing with compromise "risks his soul". It was a poignant and telling moment.

George Walker Bush talked openly about his faith— directly to me during a debate. Six Republican presidential hopefuls faced off in Des Moines in late 1999. Tom Brokaw and I co-moderated the nationally televised event. Towards the end of the debate, I asked a question selected from hundreds submitted by local viewers: "What political philosopher or thinker do you most identify with and why?"

Steve Forbes, sitting on the far left, was the first to reply. He talked at some length about John Locke and Thomas Jefferson. Next was Allen Keyes, and he also talked extensively about the founders of our country.

To the right of Keyes was George Bush, still months away from the nomination. Bush responded: "Christ, because he changed my heart." I was struck by both the answer and its brevity. After a couple of seconds of silence, I followed up: "I think the viewer would like to know more on how he (Christ) has changed your heart." To which Bush replied: " Well, it they don't know it's gonna be hard to explain. When you turn your heart and your life over to Christ, when you accept Christ as the Savior, it changes your heart and changes your life and that's what happened to me."

The exchange with Bush has become a part of political campaign history — periodically turning up in columns, books and news broadcasts even to this day. Among the early pundits, Hanna Rosin of the Washington Post wrote: "It's becoming known as Campaign 2000's 'Christ Moment'." And Howard Fineman of Newsweek penned: "I think it was an extraordinary moment where secular politics and religious faith intersected."

Some questioned Bush's sincerity, others accused him of using his faith for political purposes. What did I think? One of my immediate thoughts went something like this: "I'll bet this man doesn't realize I attended seminary — he just thinks of me as a broadcast journalist eager to derail him with a pointed question!" Little did Bush know that I was intrigued by and empathetic to his response. But I also felt uneasy about its propriety in that forum. I later agreed with several mainline church officials who warned against "professions of faith as a way to procure votes".

Yet I respect both Clinton and Bush for struggling to apply their faith to the awesome task of leading our nation. Can God work through them? Can God work through us? Does our faith really impact or inform our daily lives?

I hope the following reflections, along with biblical verses that spoke to me about the related events, will help you better connect your faith to everyday life. Our faith cannot thrive in isolation from the concerns, fears and joys of the world around us. And I pray that in your personal meditations you encounter what is profoundly true—beyond the facts.

BEYOND THE FACTS

SOCIETY AND CULTURE

SOCIETY AND CULTURE

As a news anchor, I try to understand both sides of any story. That requires a certain separation or disengagement to be impartial and fair. In some ways, it's similar to our standing as Christians—we have to be careful how engaged we become in those quarters of our world that would rather smother than kindle the Spirit.

Today's society, with its diverse and influential cultures, presents a daunting challenge and exciting opportunity for people of faith. Sometimes it is very difficult to sense God's presence in the midst of our modern concerns. At other times the Spirit moves us deeply in the unlikeliest of venues.

Come with me as we reflect on: the need for prayer even among the most powerful; the limits of family loyalty; the virtues of discipline; the individual temptations of every profession; the inadequacies of wealth; the inherent perils of merging faith and politics; the demands of true justice; and the reality of paralyzing fear—just some of life's moments freeze-framed in this first section of our spiritual exploration.

❖ ❖ ❖

PRAYER

And in the morning, a great while before day, he rose and went out to a lonely place, and there he prayed.

Mark 1:35

The President of the United States
is talking about his faith.
We're in the Roosevelt Room
of the White House.
It's early evening
on the day of the Oklahoma City bombing.
The President confides
that after first learning of the tragedy
and watching developments on television,
he turned to prayer.
Alone,
he prayed
for the victims,
their families,
and for guidance
in his response
to the nation.
"I cannot imagine
holding this office,
and its awesome responsibilities,
without faith."

We are all so busy,
constantly on the move,
immersed in noise,
shouldering our special responsibilities.
We quite simply need
more solitude
and time
to pray.

URGENT NEED

And let our people learn to apply themselves to good deeds, so as to help cases of urgent need....

Titus 3:14

International officials warn
it's reminiscent
of Rwanda
and Bosnia
and Cambodia —
mass murders,
if not genocide.
In Sudan's Darfur region,
militias are killing
unarmed civilians
as well as rebels.
Refugees are streaming
across the border.
Relief agencies
simply can't handle
this monumental crisis.
More money,
more aid,
more attention —
all are needed
immediately.

It's happening now.
We're ashamed
of past neglect,
but this is now
and regrets
are cheap
after clarion calls
are ignored.

RISK

*...men who have risked their lives for the sake of
our Lord Jesus Christ.*

Acts 15:26

He sold everything
he owned
for one Las Vegas bet.
$135,000 placed on red
at the roulette wheel.
Round and round
the wheel spins.
The ball bounces
from black
to red
to black —
finally resting on red.
With his worth
instantly doubled,
he leaves the table.
But casino officials
get his signature
to display in the lobby
to lure others
for such a gamble.
Occasionally,
we beat the odds
with the quick fix,
a short cut,
something for nothing —
in effect
taking from others.
Contrast that
to the ultimate risk
of living
for others.

QUIET SOUL

But I have calmed and quieted my soul, like a child quieted at its mother's breast; like a child that is quieted is my soul.

Psalms 131:2

Inside a restaurant
the mother
is breast-feeding
her infant.
The manager interrupts,
telling the woman
to cover up more,
move to the restroom,
or leave.
She walks out
of the establishment
where earlier this summer
women competed
in a wet T-shirt contest!

How scrambled
and disoriented
is our confused culture.
Loving tranquility
gets muddled
with lewd display.
No wonder
our souls
are uneasy.

❖ ❖ ❖

FAMILY

And looking around on those who sat about him, he said, "Here are my mother and my brothers! Whoever does the will of God is my brother, and sister, and mother."

Mark 3:34-35

A father in Turkey
has strangled his daughter —
to protect
his family's honor.
The teenage girl
had shamed her relatives
by being raped!
To save face
in such a culture
the father
throttles the life
of his own blood.

Even in our society
we elevate family
to a hallowed pedestal.
But God's demands
may at times
tear us from either
the selfish harmony
or the myopic evils
of family bonds.
Our ultimate loyalty
binds us to
what is right
and just.

❖ ❖ ❖

ENEMIES

Love your enemies, do good to those who hate you.

Luke 6:27

As a former governor
and senator,
he's telling me
about his time in office—
visceral memories,
especially that year
he nearly ran for president.
Speaking to enthusiastic crowds,
he sparked swelling support.
But prayerful reflection
stopped his campaign
with a stunning self-realization:
his beliefs
would prevent him
from ever unleashing
nuclear weapons .
Yet the nation's defense
against our enemies
demanded that posture.
He abandoned
his ambition,
but preserved
his uncompromising faith.

Rules

And he said to them, "Is it lawful on the sabbath to do good or to do harm, to save life or to kill?" But they were silent.

Mark 3:4

The teenager
has been shot
on a basketball court—
caught in gang crossfire.
Blood spurts
from his collapsed body
just yards from a hospital.
Friends beg
emergency staff inside
to come out and help.
But hospital policy
prohibits doctors and nurses
from leaving the building.
Thirty minutes later,
a confounded policeman
wheels in the boy himself.
One hour later,
the teenager dies.

We make laws
and policy—
mostly for worthy purposes.
But sometimes
the rules rule us.
We become slaves
to the regimen
rather than instruments
of the Spirit.

❖ ❖ ❖

Numbered

"Why, even the hairs of your head are all numbered."

Luke 12:7

A congressional subcommittee
is questioning
the deputy defense secretary:
"How many American troops
have died in Iraq?"
He's caught off guard
and answers incorrectly.
He underestimates
the deaths
by more than 25 percent.

In wars,
in poverty,
in natural disasters,
individuals become numbers
that can lose meaning —
except to friends
and family
and our Father.
Each one of us
lives and dies
in the embrace
of a caring
and personal Spirit.

DISCIPLINE

For the moment all discipline seems painful rather than pleasant; later it yields the peaceful fruit of righteousness to those who have been trained by it.

Hebrews 12:11

The high school principal
quashed homecoming.
Not on a whim.
Only after repeated warnings
that the toilet paper tossing
and egg smashing
had gone too far.
When dozens of students
still banded together
and plastered several teachers' homes,
the principal
canceled homecoming events —
no pep rally, no dance.
Then overnight
somebody broke the windows
of his family van.
But on the weekend
many students still danced.
Coddling parents
had arranged their own homecoming
for the kids.

Our culture of defiance
and personal gratification
begins at an early age,
nourished and fostered
often by adults.
Ignorant of imposed discipline,
how can these youngsters
ever know the fruits
of self-discipline?   ❖   ❖   ❖

POOR

"So the poor have hope, and injustice shuts her mouth."

Ezekiel 22:16

In an age
of welfare reform
one congregation has vowed
to give more than money—
they give themselves.
Members volunteer
as mentors.
They help the needy
find and keep
jobs, childcare, budgets—
the tedious basics.
They connect
and stay connected.
They are lifting
individual lives,
not the anonymous poor.
They open personal doors,
introduce possibility,
and transfuse hope.

REVENGE

"You have heard that it was said, 'An eye for an eye and a tooth for a tooth.' But I say to you...."

Matthew 5:38

When will the hideous cycle
ever end?
A young Palestinian woman,
beautiful and zealous,
trained as an attorney,
detonates a West Bank restaurant
by blowing herself up.
The suicide bombing
kills 19 other people.
What could have provoked
such brazen evil?
Israeli troops
recently killed her brother.
Eyes for eyes,
teeth for teeth,
consuming life,
obliterating hope.
The only escape
from this perpetual wickedness
is the sacred exception,
"But I say to you. . . ."
God, give us courage
to break the cycle
of revenge.

TEMPTATION

And when the devil had ended every temptation, he departed from him until an opportune time.

Luke 4:13

In the newsroom
we often wrestle
with the same dilemma:
Should we lead
tonight's broadcast
with the most significant
or the most enticing story?
The legislative vote
that will impact everyone,
or the vivid fire
that will fascinate
the largest audience?
Journalistic integrity
can handcuff
business judgment.
A noble decision today
will only be succeeded
by another tempting choice
tomorrow.

WEALTH

It is easier for a camel to go through the eye of a needle than for a rich man to enter the kingdom of God.

Mark 10:25

Prime rib.
So much prime beef
toppling each plate.
It's a charity banquet.
Good people, caring people, generous people—
wealthy people.
Dazzling diamonds,
purple cummerbunds.
Congratulatory oratory,
expansive praise
serenading all of us—
wrapped in the glow
of philanthropic contentment.
Yet,
so much prime rib
dumped back
onto waiting carts,
which soon will bring
the chocolate mousse.

APOLOGY

I confess my iniquity, I am sorry for my sin.

Psalms 38:18

On this 40th anniversary
of the Civil Rights Act,
a Southern newspaper
runs a front-page apology.
Editors regret
the paper's lack
of coverage
when it mattered
the most —
during the protests
and demonstrations
of the 1960s.
So today's editors
apologize
for their predecessors.
But what current prejudices
will require
future apologies?

Lord,
give us the wisdom
to discern
our sins
and the courage
to confess them —
now.

❖ ❖ ❖

Communion

And the Pharisees and the scribes murmured, saying,
"This man receives sinners and eats with them."

Luke 15:2

A Roman Catholic bishop
in Colorado
proclaims that communion
should be forbidden
to anyone supporting
politicians who favor
stem-cell research,
abortion rights,
and euthanasia.

Communion —
sharing,
fellowship,
inclusion,
participation.
Jesus welcomed
everyone
to the table —
in fact
he sought out
the sinners,
much less
those who disagreed
with him.
As people of faith,
we must embrace
rather than divide,
commune
rather than exclude.

❖ ❖ ❖

PUBLIC SERVANTS

Behold my servant, whom I uphold, my chosen, in whom my soul delights; I have put my Spirit upon him, he will bring forth justice to the nations.

Isaiah 42:1

A state lawmaker
is speaking
to her spellbound colleagues.
Eight months ago
she suffered a stillbirth,
losing a baby girl.
Now she's passionately lobbying
for legislative help
in the prevention
of stillbirths.
Her raw emotions
transfuse each word
and finally spill out in tears.
Fellow lawmakers,
many crossing the aisle,
offer solace and support.
They vote unanimously
in favor of the bill.

The soul of public service
is imbued with Spirit
that dissolves party lines
and nationalistic boundaries,
and delights
in compassion and concern.

Bad Fruit

"Do not be deceived; God is not mocked,
for whatever a man sows, that he will also reap."

Galatians 6:7

High in the mountains
of southwestern Poland,
a cultural revolution
divides old and young.
For decades
village women have made lace—
mostly clerical vestments
for priests and altars.
But demand for the church products
has sharply dropped.
So some younger women,
with the help of the internet,
started a thriving business.
They're using
their cherished lace-making skills
to craft G-strings!

Times and cultures change.
We adapt to provide
for our loved ones.
But society's enticements
can misguide us,
swallowing our identity
and corrupting
the harvest
of our labors.

❖ ❖ ❖

Faith and Politics

...whereas the aim of our charge is love that issues from a pure heart and a good conscience and sincere faith.

1 Timothy: 1:5

It's a presidential debate,
broadcast on national television.
I ask each candidate:
"What political philosopher
or thinker
do you most identify with, and why?"
The future president responds:
"Christ, because he changed my heart."
Some in the audience applaud,
others question
whether faith should be used
to persuade voters.
I look in his eyes,
and the intent
seems sincere.
But some see a smirk
when he is pressed to explain.
Our faith inhabits
our whole being,
yet we must isolate it
from expedience.

WALL

For he is our peace, who has made us both one,
and has broken down the dividing wall of hostility....

Ephesians 1:14

The Israelis are erecting a wall
in the West Bank.
Today they destroyed
an olive grove
to clear a path
for the wall.
It's needed,
they insist,
to prevent
Palestinian suicide bombings.
They replant
scores of the razed olive trees
on nearby soil.
But local farmers
say few will live.
Nor will
any peace
imposed by a wall.

NEIGHBOR

". . .and to love one's neighbor as oneself, is much more than all whole burnt offerings and sacrifices"

Mark 12:33

On the third night of Hanukkah,
a vandal
smashed the front window
of a suburban home,
seized the lighted menorah inside
and flung it to the ground.
In the morning,
neighbors visited
to console the family
who couldn't hide
their fear and pain.
What to do?
First one,
then another,
and now dozens
of nearby Christian families
are displaying menorahs
in their front windows.
It is a neighborhood
of reindeers,
wreaths,
nativity scenes,
and menorahs.
And the lights
this season
shine brighter
and purer than ever.

❖ ❖ ❖

JUSTICE

"But let justice roll down like waters, and righteousness like an ever-flowing stream."

Amos 5:24

She's a senior citizen
in the best sense of each word.
She's behind bars
in civil protest.
She accuses our government
of training Latin American officers
who then kill and torture
in countries ravaged by poverty.
Critics dismiss her
as naive,
but others hear her voice
as a solitary call of conscience.
Her attorney son
fears for her safety,
but the inmates
sense her virtue
and turn to her for solace.
Prophetically,
she is using the justice system
to probe and question
social justice.

❖ ❖ ❖

Punishment

And every priest stands daily at his service, offering repeatedly the same sacrifices, which can never take away sins.

Hebrews 10:11

Three inmates
who killed five people
while robbing a bank
face execution.
They're waging
a final legal battle—
labeling the electric chair
cruel and unusual
punishment.
One absurdity
begets another.
State officials respond
by changing their routine.
No longer four jolts of electricity—
now just one extended tremor!

Murders cannot
be substituted.
Violence
cannot expiate.
Deadly punishment
defaces mankind.

❖ ❖ ❖

Relationship

"A new heart I will give you,
and a new spirit I will put within you."

Ezekiel 36:26

Worshippers packed churches
in the days following
the September 11th attacks.
In sanctuaries
across the nation,
attendance soared.
Some ministers proclaimed
a spiritual renewal
of epochal proportion.
But weeks later,
many of the pews
emptied again—
the newly religious
stayed home.

Lasting faith
transcends emotional lifelines.
The Spirit
wants to envelop
the heart,
and thrives
in a deep
two-way relationship.

FEAR

Fear not, for I am with you.

Isaiah 41:10

September 11th.
Terrifying, hideous, brutal murder.
For thousands of families,
utter despair.
For countless others,
agonizing fear.
The horrific images,
searingly transmitted
on that brilliant blue day,
ushered in
a new age of anxiety.
We seek refuge
in God's assurances,
even as some
curse a God
who could allow such evil.

God has no remote control.
Yet we sense
divine presence
in the arms of the rescuers
and the resolve of recovery.
That spiritual presence,
that shared mystery,
passes all understanding
and sustains us
as we face our fears.

BEYOND THE FACTS

SIN

SIN

One of the journalist's most important roles is that of watchdog. It's part of our job to identify a corrupt government official or businessman. We're supposed to highlight what's wrong so it can be corrected! Ideally, we're helping to protect the public. But often viewers question our emphasis on the negative. Unfortunately, misconduct emerges nearly everywhere we look.

Human sin strains our relationship with God. Nothing that we do can cause God to abandon us, but our personal failures often disrupt the spiritual connections that nurture our well-being. We may feel anxious and alone, not because of God's retreat, but because of our shameful and alienating behavior.

The daily misdeeds range from the unkind to the criminal, but their spiraling impact can be surprisingly destructive: simple anger can disrupt into dangerous hatred; greedy consumption becomes the accepted norm; spouses ignore the devastating impact of their actions on their loved-one; and we fall off the tightrope between enabling and impairing the young. But no matter how far we may distance ourselves from God, we are still called to a new humanity, and we are never forgotten.

❖ ❖ ❖

ANGER

Be angry but do not sin; do not let the sun go down on your anger, and give no opportunity to the devil.

Ephesians 4:26-27

The judge's order
forbids the woman
from going anywhere
near the radio station.
Police say
she was angered
by the opinions
broadcast in a talk show.
She fired shots
at the station's building
and parking lot.
Now she faces
criminal charges.

Anger
can motivate us
or destroy us.
How do we channel
our emotions
effectively?
Father,
may our convictions
energize us
to create
rather than dismantle,
to mend
not mangle,
to unify
not divide.

❖ ❖ ❖

Gifts

Now there are varieties of gifts, but the same Spirit; and there are varieties of service, but the same Lord; and there are varieties of working, but it is the same God who inspires them all in every one.

1 Corinthians 12:4-5

The professional boxer
has fought his last fight—
a fatal bout.
He flattened his opponent,
who fell into unconsciousness
and two days later died.
The boxer
is a church deacon.
He now says
he will never hit
another man.

Each of us
is blessed
with diverse gifts.
But what is the fount
of those gifts?
Are they God's gifts?
Do we share them in service?
Is the Spirit guiding
our achievements?

❖ ❖ ❖

MOVING FORWARD

*...but one thing I do, forgetting what lies behind
and straining forward to what lies ahead....*

Philippians 3:13

He's been in prison
nearly 30 years.
He started an apartment fire
that killed five people.
The jury convicted him
of murder.
Evidence suggested
he set the fire on purpose.
New evidence
suggests otherwise.
He always claimed
he was simply trying
to light a cigarette
in a drunken stupor.
Now the parole board
is hearing his appeal
for freedom.
Character witnesses
praise his prison behavior.
But when asked
to name his victims,
he admits
he has forgotten.

To move on,
some things we must forget.
Others,
we must always remember.
Help us, Lord,
to know the difference.

❖ ❖ ❖

HYPOCRITES

*"You hypocrites! Well did Isaiah prophesy of you,
when he said: 'This people honors me with their lips,
but their heart is far from me"*

Matthew 15:7-8

She's sitting at home
nursing a cold.
Famous as a brassy comedienne,
she's surprisingly serene
as we begin the interview.
Calmly she describes
her stormy past —
ravaged by alcohol,
drugs, and sex abuse.
She's a survivor.
But the real insight
comes when I ask about
the root of her humor:
"I love taking shots
at snooty hypocrites,
though I'm the master of them all!
Comedy is supposed
to hurt and heal."

The prophetic critique
carries a wicked jab
injuring each of us.
Fortunately,
God's grace heals
the humbled heart.

❖ ❖ ❖

IMPENITENT

They have made their faces harder than rock;
they have refused to repent.

Jeremiah 5:3

The convicted killer
dispassionately awaits
his formal sentencing.
Also in the courtroom,
the families of his two victims.
They are about to read
victim impact statements —
their one chance
to painfully explain
the immeasurable suffering
inflicted by the killer.
But unexpectedly
defense attorneys request
and the judge allows
the murderer
to leave the courtroom
to shield himself
from the dreadful effects
of his own odious deeds.

When we avoid
the grievous consequences,
when we reject
the Spirit's power
of redemption,
given true remorse,
we are condemned
to hopelessness.

❖ ❖ ❖

THIEF

"While you preach against stealing, do you steal?"

Romans 2:21

The call comes to police
late at night—
strange and suspicious noises
in the middle of a field.
Officers speed to the scene.
They find two men
using a crow bar and hammer
trying to open a safe
they had stolen
from a fraternal lodge.
The bungling bandits
managed only
to snap off
the safe's handle.
The cash is untouched.

We may ridicule
such blatantly foolish thieves,
such futile greed;
yet how easily we slip
into accepted behavior
of lavish acquisition
and mindless waste,
consuming so much more
than we merit.
Are we stealing
from God's bounty?

SUBHUMAN

...your iniquities have made a separation
between you and your God....

Isaiah 59:2

The appalling pictures
show American soldiers
torturing
and humiliating
Iraqi prisoners.
Other horrifying video
displays Iraqi militants
beheading hostages.
War's wretched evils
unmask man's
darkest nature—
we perversely degenerate
into the subhuman!
By excluding God,
we destroy
any semblance
of our intended humanity.
We descend
into the hopeless hell
of separation.

Becoming One

*"...a man shall leave his father and mother
and be joined to his wife, and the two shall become one."*

Mark 10:7-8

The jury convicted him today.
Guilty of murder.
He killed
a neighboring farmer
over a land dispute.
One victim
now multiplied —
two families
devastated by the act.
In the courtroom,
the murderer's wife
is wracked with crippling emotion,
the same contortions
I saw months earlier
when she accompanied him
for an interview.
We televised her husband,
but I couldn't help sensing
the debilitating grief,
the profound sadness
that enwrapped
her whole being
as she sat silently nearby.

Do those of us
who have become one
fully comprehend
the dreadful pain
we can inflict on
our other half?

❖ ❖ ❖

COACHING

...you then who teach others, will you not teach yourself?

Romans 2:21

The teacher-coach
is apologizing
to a student
in front of
the entire school.
This after the young teacher
embarrassed the honor student,
an average basketball player,
by publicly presenting him
a Crybaby Award
at a team banquet.
The student's offense?
Imploring to play
in games.
Now the school
has named a new award
after the student,
honoring his effort
and spirit.

Teaching is so noble,
so crucial,
so enhancing —
yet fraught
with risks and peril.
The teacher,
with the student,
is always learning.

Removed From God

...for the anger of man does not work the righteousness of God.

James 1:20

More than 20 angry men,
mostly fathers,
leap from the bleachers
and rush onto the baseball diamond.
Yelling and cursing,
they flail wildly
at each other.
Wide-eyed youngsters,
four and five-year-olds,
stand transfixed.
All this
over a disputed call
in a T-ball game!

Fits of anger,
tempers exploding,
outrageous foolishness exposed.
Whether we're screaming
at some "idiot" driver
or our own wayward child,
we should pause
and understand
we're acting alone,
removed from God.

❖ ❖ ❖

WEAKNESS OF GOD

...but we preach Christ crucified....For the foolishness of God is wiser than men, and the weakness of God is stronger than men.
                                                    1 Corinthians 1:23,25

As a teenager,
he survived the horrors
of a German labor camp.
Now he speaks
to American teens
so they will never forget
the atrocities he witnessed
and suffered.
But of the memories he shares,
one is unexpected:
after liberation,
in a nearby town,
several former prisoners
recognize a hated voice —
and descend
on the man
who had been a despicable guard
and kill him.

It's certainly understandable.
The natural reaction.
Naturally human.
But the cross
reveals and empowers
a new humanity.

❖ ❖ ❖

Never Forgotten

"Can a woman forget her sucking child, that she should have no compassion on the son of her womb? Even these may forget, yet I will not forget you."

Isaiah 49:15

How could it happen?
A loving mother,
confused by a new family routine,
drops off her young son at day care—
but then forgets
to take her baby daughter
to the sitter's house,
and unknowingly
leaves the infant
in the back seat
of the sealed van.
Temperatures inside soar.
Consumed by her work,
the mother only later
makes the horrifying discovery.
The heat has sucked the life
from her beautiful daughter.

Appearing before cameras,
mother and father
are drained too of all life.
Wracked with grief,
they barely utter
a few words
through choked tears.
It is too agonizing
to watch,
and clearly unbearable
to experience.
Yet,
they are not forgotten.

❖ ❖ ❖

BEYOND THE FACTS

FATE

FATE

I do tire of emphasizing the tragic, but that is often the reality of the unusual and the unexpected, which, after all, is news. Admittedly, a corrosive outcome of our approach is inordinate apprehension. Dwelling on disaster makes it seem more likely — that can be unhealthy for all of us.

But the disturbing truth is that our world features considerable misfortune and tragedy. Even worse, those events often victimize the blameless. For many people, that is the most persistent and persuasive argument against faith. How could a loving God allow such cruel perversity?

The tornado capriciously kills one and spares another; tsunamis devastate entire countries; some wives see their husbands return from war, others do not; a social worker, who knows only how to help, is gunned down; a young man wrongly imprisoned is incapable of recapturing his lost years. Life is not predictable or fair. Deep sighs accompany any shouts of joy. Yet, mysteriously, God's blessings are not silenced. We must seize, share, and celebrate those blessings before our precious moments in this life are spent.

❖ ❖ ❖

WORSE OFFENDERS

"Or those eighteen upon whom the tower in Siloam fell and killed them, do you think that they were worse offenders than all the others who dwelt in Jerusalem?"

Luke 13:4

The twister tears
through the small town,
destroying a community building.
Inside,
four women
who operate a food pantry
one day a month.
This is that one day.
The tornado kills
two of the women
and injures the other two.
Residents shake their heads,
and some shake their fists—
it doesn't make sense.
No platitudes will help.
But reality sharpens
our perspective,
deflating the sanctimonious.
Fate has no moral favorites.

SPIRIT'S WAY

"What man of you, having a hundred sheep, if he has lost one of them, does not leave the ninety-nine in the wilderness, and go after the one which is lost, until he finds it?"

Luke 15:4

The tsunami disaster
across southern Asia
numbs the mind.
Death toll numbers
wash in
like tidal waves themselves.
It's impossible
to grasp
the breadth of the tragedy
until we see the pictures
of individual horror
and anguish—
surviving parents
wandering coastlines
hopelessly looking
for their children
swallowed by the waters
days before.

Mass humanity
is an empty
expressionless image—
much like that of
a distant,
omnipotent God.
The Spirit's way
connects personally,
individually, purposefully.
God's sorrow
is not blanketed—
it is shared
tear by tear.

❖ ❖ ❖

SUFFERING

How long must I bear pain in my soul, and have sorrow in my heart all the day?...lighten my eyes, lest I sleep the sleep of death.

Psalms 13:2,3

An elderly couple is dead.
Her body had been ravaged
by lung cancer.
Doctors offered no hope.
He couldn't bear
her pain.
In the hospital room,
he leaned near her,
whispering soft words.
He lifted a gun
and fired
at her
and then himself.

Suffering can starve
all hope.
It can suffocate
and blind.
Oh God,
lighten the eyes
that cannot see
before or beyond
death.

THE LIGHT

"Walk while you have the light, lest darkness overtake you...believe in the light, that you may become sons of light."

John 12:35-36

A brain tumor
gradually devours
his once keen intellect.
A nurse tries to assess the loss,
administering a simple test:
"Name the months in order."
He strains to recall
and drops his head
in failure.
Later his daughter-in-law
silently enters his room
and finds him
desperately studying a calendar.

Darkness
eventually descends
on all of us.
But God's light
is eternal
and demands
no final test.

SIGHS

...for we do not know how to pray as we ought, but the Spirit himself intercedes for us with sighs too deep for words.

Romans 8:26

Widows of fallen soldiers,
they've become
a suffering sisterhood.
Their husbands,
from the same Army division,
died fighting in Iraq.
For a time,
they still bonded with other wives,
waiting for loved ones to return.
But now those soldiers
are coming home
to tiptoed hugs
and joyful celebrations.
The contrasting silence
echoes in shadows
through the widows' sleepless nights.
No words.
Only sighs,
soaked with emotions
impossible to speak.
Yet the Spirit
is felt.

DISTURBED

But Jesus rebuked him, saying, "Be silent, and come out of him!" And the unclean spirit, convulsing him and crying with a loud voice, came out of him.

Mark 1:25-26

A middle-aged woman
faces time in prison
and treatment
for mental illness.
She inflicted terrible pain
on the parents
of a young girl
who disappeared
nearly 20 years ago.
She pretended to be
their daughter,
miraculously surfacing
after all these years.
For the couple,
ecstatic joy
burst quickly
into familiar despair.
Police say the woman
has exhibited
multiple personalities.

Disturbed minds,
frightening and injurious,
distant and lost.
Yet, sometimes
the Spirit connects,
clearing the psychotic cobwebs,
providing peace.
Surely
we too are
within reach!

❖ ❖ ❖

Why

Precious in the sight of the Lord is the death of his saints.

Psalms 116:15

His death provokes
all the agonizing questions
that unsettle our minds
whenever good seems punished.
As a social worker
he gave hope and direction
to so many troubled lives.
Loving father of six children,
he cherished their futures.
Yet a teenage client
has senselessly gunned him down.
The response overwhelms.
Men cry and women weep
in loving recollections
of his boundless heart.
The outpouring
instills a visceral determination
in the rest of us
to somehow preserve
that same sense of hope—
despite the seemingly
unanswered despair.
Our response
is profoundly critical.

TIME

For everything there is a season, and a time for every matter under heaven: a time to be born, and a time to die....

Ecclesiastes 3:1-2

How can a heart
be so heavy,
and yet still dance?
Last week he lost
his beloved wife
to cancer.
Today he rejoices
in the birth
of his first grandson.
The mystery of time.
God's gift
and burden.
The twinkling of an eye,
the endless shadows of grief.
In joy,
there is no clock.
In sorrow,
there is no tomorrow.
No answers,
only more questions.
But for now,
one question
might lead to an answer:
Are we truly living
each moment?

❖ ❖ ❖

BLAMELESS

"I am blameless...."

Job 9:21

As a 17-year-old,
he was convicted
of rape and murder.
"I'm innocent,"
he always claimed.
After 27 years in prison,
DNA tests proved him right.
At first he reveled
in the intoxicating freedom.
Now the reality
of lost time
and relationships
and achievements
haunts his life.
Today he strains
to detect
even a shadow
of hope.

When fate slaps us
with misfortune,
we often slide
into the self-absorption
of our miseries.
Wake us, Lord,
from our self-pity,
and restore
the delight
in our freedom
to be.

❖ ❖ ❖

COMPLACENCY

*"...you are always with me,
and everything that I have is yours."*

Luke 15:31

Empty,
repetitive days,
adrift in boredom,
relishing nothing,
bypassing life's pulsating verve.

Then the doctor says
he needs to take a biopsy
of your wife's breast.
Days of wrenching anxiety
finally dissolve with the word "benign."
Death's specter
has shaken us awake.
We inhale the morning breeze,
luxuriate in the massaging sunlight,
and tremble at our loved one's touch.
For these precious weeks,
we are centered in the divine—
we see keenly.
We savor
each simple gift.
But, gradually, we turn away—
seeking even more,
not realizing our loss.

BLESSED

"Blessed are the eyes which see what you see!."

Luke 10:23

The infant has only known
intensive care
since birth.
Tied by tubes
to various machines,
she is still breathing.
Each day is a gift.
Her grandfather,
a beloved professor,
speaks about
the widening circle of love.
Thirty of his students
independently offered
to donate their blood.
He mentions
the phone calls,
the cards,
the prayers,
and the tireless, loving care
of countless nurses and doctors—
God's healing work
through human hands.
The granddaughter
may live
or die.
But the widening circle of love
blesses all who see.

❖ ❖ ❖

BEYOND THE FACTS

INSPIRATION

Inspiration

My career is now well into its fourth decade, and I've been fortunate enough to rub shoulders with scores of famous and influential people. But I've been touched emotionally most often by those uncelebrated individuals who quietly and sincerely seem moved by God to enhance the lives of those around them.

Each day brings inspiring stories that uplift and encourage us. We can never escape life's dark and grievous turns, but God's presence empowers us to move forward with hope and resilience. The Spirit guides our response to misfortune and evil, transforming us into a new creation.

A minister rescues a prostitute from the streets; a newspaper editor bravely exposes drug traffickers; parents lose their son but challenge his classmates; a black physician heals a white community; young offenders make the most of a second chance; an elderly man saves yet another life. We are deeply moved by the dynamic force of the enabling Spirit. Accept it with wonder!

❖ ❖ ❖

NEW CREATION

Therefore, if any one is in Christ, he is a new creation; the old has passed away, behold, the new has come.

2 Corinthians 5:17

He helps the homeless.
He's savvy;
he knows the streets.
Early on
he began providing
transitional housing
for homeless mothers and children.
Now the ministry
includes some permanent housing.
He's rescued
several hundred children
from shelters.
No stranger
to disappointment and betrayal,
he rejoices in the miracles—
like the prostitute
he confronted years ago.
"You are a creation of God,"
he told her.
To his amazement,
those simple words
struck a resonant chord.
She stopped selling
her body.
She regained custody
of her daughter.
She was transformed
into a new creation
and remains so even today.

❖ ❖ ❖

ALIVE

"You blind guides, straining out a gnat and swallowing a camel!"

Matthew 23:24

Special ceremonies,
attended by the First Lady,
honor the high school
history teacher.
What's his secret?
Students,
administrators,
and fellow teachers agree:
with fascinating facts
and compelling stories
he animates
the chronicled figures
of each era —
they become real
and sympathetic.

Jesus' vigor
and graphic eloquence
and robust convictions
reflect a vibrant being,
not a lifeless icon.
To confront
that real person
deepens and colors
my understanding
of the living Spirit.

❖ ❖ ❖

COURAGE

...we had courage in our God to declare to you the gospel of God in the face of great opposition.

1 Thessalonians 2:2

He edited a newspaper
that boldly exposed
drug traffickers
in Mexico.
The reports spotlighted
the malignancy
of the narcotics deals.
Walking today
with his two young children,
he was gunned down
by masked killers
in a passing truck.

The courage
to speak the truth
in the face
of fright,
even terror. —
Lord,
give us that voice.
Our courage
can come from you —
the courage
in our God.

SILENCED

...the whole multitude of the disciples began to rejoice and praise God....And some of the Pharisees in the multitude said to him, "Teacher, rebuke your disciples." He answered, "I tell you, if these were silent, the very stones would cry out."

Luke 19:37,39

All across campus
the bells chimed
each night
between eight and nine.
Tonight,
for the first time
in decades,
the bells
are silenced.
The university carillonneur
has died
of a stroke.
He may not be replaced;
officials point
to tight budgets.
But the joyful praise
of the Spirit
cannot be silenced.
Everything that breathes,
much less the stones,
would cry out!
The life-giving force
that dances
in eternal melody
stirs us
to become whole.

❖ ❖ ❖

DOING

...he was met by ten lepers, who stood at a distance and lifted up their voices and said, "Jesus, Master, have mercy on us." When he saw them he said to them, "Go and show yourselves to the priests." And as they went they were cleansed.

Luke 17:12-14

Exposing college students
to charity work!
Organizers are awarding
coveted concert tickets
to those who contribute
10 volunteer hours.
It's in the doing —
helping the disabled,
assisting a food bank —
that the students
surprise themselves
by realizing
the benefits firsthand.

So too our faith
resonates for us
and for others
through practice
more than speculation
or endless debate.
When we follow
our Lord's will,
we open our lives
to his healing.
"As they went
they were cleansed."

❖ ❖ ❖

BEAUTY

"Why this waste? For this ointment might have been sold for a large sum, and given to the poor." But Jesus, aware of this, said to them, "Why do you trouble the woman? For she has done a beautiful thing to me."

Matthew 26:8-10

Budget cuts
threaten to strangle
the city's public schools.
Could a recent find
offer an easy solution?
Hundreds of valuable art pieces
had been stored away
for decades.
Appraisers say
the paintings
and sculptures
and tapestries
could profit the school system
millions of dollars.
But officials,
rejecting the proposal,
talk of proudly displaying
the works
so children
can learn to appreciate
and enjoy.

Something inherent
in the creative process
mysteriously resembles
the enabling Spirit.
To strive
for authentic beauty
and then share it,
approaches
a sacred purity
and reflects the sublime.

❖ ❖ ❖

Sprouting

*He said therefore, "What is the kingdom of God like?
And to what shall I compare it? It is like a grain of mustard
seed which a man took and sowed in his garden; and it grew
and became a tree, and the birds of the air made nests
in its branches."*

Luke 13:18-19

He would have graduated
from high school
this week.
But three years ago
he died
of an enlarged heart.
His parents
are giving each classmate
a $10 experiment.
Use the money,
they're urging,
to touch someone else
with kindness —
as their loving son
might have done.
Imagine what could result
if these small gifts
blossom into
untold generosity.

God's values
will always thrive,
offering solace
and shelter
from the world's
withering expedience.

❖ ❖ ❖

Faithful Finish

I have fought the good fight, I have finished the race,
I have kept the faith.

2 Timothy 4:7

It's the state high school
cross country championship meet,
and two teammates
are just 400 meters
from the finish line
and victory.
But suddenly one pulls up,
exhausted,
unable to go on.
Without hesitation,
the other reaches out to help,
and awkwardly
they limp to the finish.
Together they cross —
both disqualified.

No garlands,
no wreaths,
no trophies.
no titles,
and no regrets.
Instead,
an instinctive sense
of ultimate purpose
in life's constant race.

❖ ❖ ❖

S℘EAKING CLEARLY

...that I may make it clear, as I ought to speak.

Colossians 4:4

The Great Communicator
has died.
I interviewed him
three years
after he left
the Oval Office.
We talked about
his early career
as a broadcaster
at the radio station
that preceded
my television station.
He reminisced,
without any signs
of Alzheimer's disease.
He regaled me
with spirited stories,
each featuring
one telling point
or punch line!
Affable,
genuine,
engaging,
direct,
persuasive.
Sometimes
most of us
get lost
in complicated nuance,
and fail
to communicate
the spiritual essence.

❖   ❖   ❖

TREASURE

"For where your treasure is, there will your heart be also."

Matthew 6:21

She loves poetry.
For years she submitted
her own poems
to a national literary magazine.
Editors always rejected
her work —
even though she's a billionaire.
Still she composed,
and found other avenues
to cultivate poetry.
Through the magazine
she contributed prizes
and literary fellowships.
Now she's revised her will
and the periodical,
which still hasn't published her verse,
will receive a generous portion
of her fortune.
She's investing
her prosaic treasures
in a heartfelt
and spiritual conviction.

❖ ❖ ❖

Response

"Just so, I tell you, there is joy before the angels of God over one sinner who repents."

Luke 15:10

Decades ago,
the couple ran a restaurant.
Among their Christmas mail
this year—
a letter containing
five $100 bills.
With the money,
a poignant note
from a former employee
apologizing for his thievery
those many years ago.
Their reaction?
Celebration,
satisfaction,
and a donation.
Some friends suggest
pursuit and prosecution—
perhaps recovering
much more money.
But this couple
savors too much
the human remorse,
to defile it
with other than
an angelic response.

❖ ❖ ❖

Personal God

And because you are sons, God has sent the Spirit of his Son

into our hearts, crying , "Abba! Father!"

Galatians 4:6

The national media spotlight
focused on her for days.
A neonatalogist,
she helped deliver septuplets.
She shared her faith
with the world,
telling reporters afterwards:
"God is not abstract."
Much later,
I ask her what she meant.
"God cares about individuals."
She reveals
a personal bout
of clinical depression
during medical school.
"God never lifted his hand from me."
She recovered,
stronger for the experience,
prepared for future challenges—
like high-profile pregnancies.
Not some abstract concept,
God is the Father,
present and personal,
for you and me.

❖ ❖ ❖

Majestic Work

When I look at thy heavens, the work of thy fingers, the moon and the stars which thou hast established; what is man that thou art mindful of him....?

Psalms 8:3

An international team
of astronomers
has just expanded
our known boundaries.
The astrophysicists
have spotted a galaxy
more than 13 billion light-years away.
That's farther away
than anything
previously discovered.
It dates back
to near the beginning
of the universe.
Well, perhaps
within 470 million years!
Our minds
flounder to grasp
the magnitude of such majesty.
Yet we are one
with the Mind
that fills the universe.

LOVE

Love bears all things, believes all things,
hopes all things, endures all things.

1 Corinthians 13:7

The fire alarm sounds,
so the teacher
leads her young students outside—
only to be attacked
by a hail of bullets.
She dives to shield
a screaming youngster.
The little girl
escapes without injury,
but her teacher
dies at the hospital.
Also killed—
four other children.
Police arrest a former student
and his young accomplice.

She relished teaching,
eager each day
to encourage,
to enable,
to truly love.
Even the difficult kids
were drawn to her,
touched by her—
or so it seemed.
She believed in them,
hoped in them.
Will her gift endure?

❖ ❖ ❖

SECOND CHANCE

"Sin no more, that nothing worse befall you."

John 5:14

A courtroom brightened
on all sides
with handshakes and hugs.
Two years ago
this group of teens,
guilty of thefts
and drug use
and fights,
faced lengthy prison terms.
Instead,
they were given
a second chance:
"Finish high school,
undergo counseling,
get a job,
do community service —
then we'll talk."
Today they're talking,
and smiling confidently,
program completed.
One more year
without offenses
and their records
will be wiped clean.

Why does it work?
More than forgiveness,
it's a directive,
and they buy into it.
They believe
with help
they can change
their lives.

❖   ❖   ❖

DECENCY

I know that it is well with your soul.

3 John 1:2

The presidential hopeful
is pulling out
of his party's race.
A veteran congressman,
he waged
a principled campaign.
reflective of his career.
But he never ignited the polls.
With his exit,
even opponents
quickly praise his character.
A "good and decent" man
is the universal plaudit.
A lethal tag
in today's explosively charged
political arena?
The congressman,
enveloped by family
and choked with emotion,
speaks from the heart—
he speaks from his soul,
which clearly is at peace.
Despite the defeat,
deep inside,
all is well.

COMPASSION

...and he had compassion on them, and healed their sick."

Matthew 14:14

He arrived
in the small town
more than four decades ago —
a black physician
in a white community.
He struggled
to establish his practice,
encountering distrust
and fear
and even hate.
He answered it all
with compassion.
Day after day
he relieved pain,
diagnosed dangers,
eased fright,
delivered new life,
and prepared for death.
Today
he's retiring.
Some patients weep,
most are saddened,
all have been healed.

Coming of Age

*"...nor do we know who opened his eyes. Ask him; he is of age,
he will speak for himself."*

John 9:21

A teenager
on the internet,
examining pictures of missing children,
suddenly, shockingly
sees himself.
According to the website,
the photo shows him
as a three-year-old
soon after his mother
had seized him
from his father's custody.
He tells a teacher,
who tells police,
who arrest his mom.
Authorities say the teenager
is distraught
when they take her away.

As we mature
our understanding
of the world
of our loved ones
and of ourselves
necessarily evolves.
Help us, Lord, to find
our own voice
and wisdom
and strength.

❖ ❖ ❖

UNDERSTANDING

"...lest they see with their eyes, and hear with their ears, and understand with their heart, and turn and be healed."

Isaiah 6:10

The three-year-old Arab girl
has a new life.
Born with a faulty heart,
she's been given
the heart of a Jewish boy.
The eight-year-old
died riding his bike,
struck by a car.
Israeli surgeons performed
the transplant.
Arabs and Jews alike
monitored the story,
following each development,
seeing with their eyes,
hearing with their ears.
The two families
have shared tears and hugs.
Now the young girl
is healing.
So, perhaps,
are others
through the understanding
of their own hearts.

❖ ❖ ❖

Family of Believers

"I know my own and my own know me,
as the Father knows me and I know the Father...."

John 10:14

The mother's belief
defied logic.
How could she know
the six-year-old girl
she'd just met
at a children's party
was her daughter —
the daughter thought to have died
as an infant in a house fire?
Gathering several strands
of the girl's hair,
the mother managed
to get them tested for DNA.
The results astounded officials.
A family acquaintance
now stands accused
of taking the baby
and torching the house
to hide the kidnapping.
The mother and daughter
have been reunited.

Our instinctive bonds,
the inherent familial ties,
originate from God our Father,
the creative source,
and resonate spiritually
in the global family
of all believers.

❖ ❖ ❖

LIFELONG WAY

Teach me, O Lord, the way of thy statutes;
and I will keep it to the end.

Psalm 119:33

He's 92 years old,
and he's done it again —
helped save a life.
Driving over a bridge,
he spotted someone
threatening to jump.
Rushing out of the car,
he joins another man
in pulling the disturbed soul
from the edge.
Eight decades ago,
this seasoned saint
saved a baby
from a blazing building.

For some,
O Lord,
your way becomes
their lifelong way.
Ingrained,
spontaneous,
expressive
in purpose and deed —
a directional beacon
for so many
wayward beings.

❖ ❖ ❖

SAVING SPIRIT

"But the Counselor, the Holy Spirit, whom the Father will send in my name, he will teach you all things...my peace I give to you."

John 14:26,27

He's an elite athlete,
a champion jockey —
third in career wins.
But his most meaningful moment
came 20 years ago.
Alone in a hotel room,
adrift in a vacuous
and self-indulgent life,
lost and depressed,
he confronted
a powerful presence.
Sensing comfort
and bearing,
he opened his heart.
For two decades now
he's relished
the Lord's Spirit,
and tirelessly promotes
track chaplaincy programs
as he races horses
across the country
to the winner's circle.

Lord,
your saving Spirit
can transform
our bleak
and hollow moments —
turning desolation
and despair
into lifelong direction
and peace.

❖ ❖ ❖

SAVING OTHERS

*"He saved others; he cannot save himself.
He is the King of Israel; let him come down now
from the cross, and we will believe in him."*

Matthew 27:42

As a gifted minister,
beloved husband,
cherished father,
he transformed
so many lives —
personifying the Spirit
and lovingly channeling
God's saving grace.
But he died today.

It is the essence
of God's love
to enliven others,
to sacrifice self,
to share the Spirit.
Because inherent
in life's cycle,
we nurture outwards.
In the end,
we are able
and are meant
to help save others,
but we cannot
save ourselves.

❖ ❖ ❖

WONDER

"...stop and consider the wondrous works of God."

Job 37:14

A professional magician,
he charmed audiences
by staging the spectacular
on television and Broadway.
He introduced magic
to a whole new generation.
His obituaries this week
speak of a genius
who excelled in illusion
and encouraged wonder.

As we age,
our cynical lens
can cloud
the real wonders.
Who needs illusion
during defining moments?
Remember
lifting your children
above the water's surface,
raising them high
against the azure sky,
and the sun shimmering
with each giggling splash?
Wondrous works indeed!